Just A Friend Coupon

giftables™

A division of Victory House, Inc.
Tulsa, Oklahoma

All Scriptures are taken from the King James Version of the Holy Bible.

JUST FOR MY FRIEND COUPONS
Copyright © 1997 by Victory House, Inc.
Cover design © 1997 by Victory House, Inc.
ISBN: 0-932081-55-X
Printed in the United States of America

Published by Victory House, Inc., P.O. Box 700238, Tulsa, Oklahoma 74170
(918) 747-5009

All rights reserved under International Copyright Law. Contents and/or cover may not be reproduced in whole or in part, in any form, or by any electronic means, including information and retrieval systems — except in the case of brief quotations embodied in critical articles or reviews — without the express written consent of the publisher.

Giftables, *giftables* logo, and gift box ■ logo are trademarks of Victory House, Inc.

Cover Design by: *Whitley Graphics*.

Active Listening Coupon. *The holder of this coupon is entitled to my listening ear. I will endeavor to be there for you when you need to talk.*

Just for My Friend
COUPON

My personal gift to _____ From _____

Special notes _____

_____

"A friend is one who is there to care"
(Anonymous).

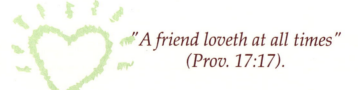

"A friend loveth at all times"
(Prov. 17:17).

Just for My Friend COUPON

The Help-With-Housework Coupon. *The holder of this coupon is entitled to my help with your housework on a mutually agreed-upon Saturday morning.*

My personal gift to _____ From _____

Special notes _____

_____

"Genuine friendship is like sound health;
its value is seldom known until it is lost"
(Anonymous).

"Love is the fulfilling of the law"
(Rom. 13:10).

I'll-Stand-By-You Coupon. *The holder of this coupon is entitled to my personal support in helping to see you through a difficult time.*

Just for My Friend COUPON

My personal gift to _____ From _____

Special notes _____

_____

"A task worth doing and friends worth having make life worthwhile"
(Anonymous).

"Though I speak with the tongues of men and of angels, and have not charity [love], I am become as sounding brass, or a tinkling cymbal"
(1 Cor. 13:1).

Just for My Friend COUPON

__A-Friend-In-Need Coupon__. The holder of this coupon is entitled to know that I will be a friend to you during your time of need.

My personal gift to _____ From _____

Special notes _____

_____

"A friend in need is a friend indeed" (Anonymous).

"And yet shew I unto you a more excellent way"
(1 Cor. 12:31).

The Call-Me-Collect Coupon.
The holder of this coupon is entitled to call me and reverse the charges on an evening of your choice when you need to talk.

Just for My Friend
COUPON

My personal gift to _____ From _____

Special notes _____

_____

"A loyal friend is someone who sticks up for you even when you're not there"
(Anonymous).

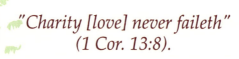

"Charity [love] never faileth"
(1 Cor. 13:8).

Just for My Friend
COUPON

The Kids-Day-Out Coupon. *The holder of this coupon is entitled to a day off from all child-care responsibilities.*

My personal gift to _____ From _____

Special notes _____

_____

"While we try to teach our children all about life, our children teach us what life is all about" (Anonymous).

"Children are an heritage of the Lord"
(Ps. 127:3).

The Tea-And-Me Coupon. *The holder of this coupon is entitled to a quiet afternoon of tea and cookies in my home with me.*

Just for My Friend
COUPON

My personal gift to _____ From _____

Special notes _____

_____

"The best vitamin for making friends is B-1" (Anonymous).

"The fruit of the Spirit is love"
(Gal. 5:22).

***The Movie-Matinee Coupon.** The holder of this coupon is entitled to select an afternoon movie that we can attend together. The movie and the popcorn are on me!*

Just for My Friend
COUPON

My personal gift to _____ From _____

Special notes _____

_____

"Friendship is a living thing that lasts only as long as it is nourished with kindness, sympathy, and understanding" (Anonymous).

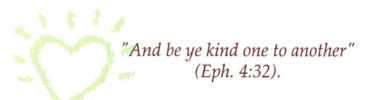

"And be ye kind one to another"
(Eph. 4:32).

Just for My Friend COUPON

A Walk-In-The-Mall Coupon.
The holder of this coupon is entitled to a Saturday afternoon of window-shopping with me in the mall of your choice. A surprise gift awaits you!

My personal gift to _____ From _____

Special notes _____

_____

"Friendships will last if they are put first" (Anonymous).

"Walk in love"
(Eph. 5:2).

I-Want-To-Help-You Coupon. *The holder of this coupon is entitled to my help with any project or special occasion that you are responsible for.*

Just for My Friend
COUPON

My personal gift to _____ From _____

Special notes _____

_____

"A true friend is like a good book –
the inside is better than the cover"
(Anonymous).

"With good will doing service, as to the Lord"
(Eph. 6:7).

Just for My Friend COUPON

The Open-Door Coupon. *The holder of this coupon is entitled to come to my home at any time, for any reason.*

My personal gift to _____ From _____

Special notes _____

_____

"A trusted friend thinks you are a good egg – even though you may be slightly cracked" (Anonymous).

"Submitting yourselves one to another in the fear of God" (Eph. 5:21).

The You-Are-Important-To-Me Coupon. *The holder of this coupon is entitled to know that I consider you to be a very special person whom I believe in and enjoy being with.*

Just for My Friend
COUPON

My personal gift to _____ From _____

Special notes _____

_____

"The best thing one friend can do for another is to refrain from giving advice" (Anonymous).

"Grace and peace be multiplied unto you through the knowledge of God" (2 Pet. 1:2).

Just for My Friend COUPON

Soft-Shoulder Coupon. *The holder of this coupon is entitled to the use of my shoulder to lean on or cry on during any time of personal crisis.*

My personal gift to _____ From _____

Special notes _____

_____

"The ornaments of a house
are the friends who frequent it"
(Anonymous).

*"Bear ye one another's burdens,
and so fulfil the law of Christ"
(Gal. 6:2).*

The Prayer-Support Coupon. *The holder of this coupon is entitled to my prayer support in any area of personal need you would like me to pray about. Your prayer request:*

_____
_____

Just for My Friend
COUPON

My personal gift to _____ From _____

Special notes _____

_____

"God never tires of hearing us in prayer"
(Anonymous).

"But my God shall supply all your need according to his riches in glory by Christ Jesus"
(Phil. 4:19).

Just for My Friend COUPON

The Movie-Matinee Coupon. *The holder of this coupon is entitled to select an afternoon movie that we can attend together. The movie and the popcorn are on me!*

My personal gift to _____ From _____

Special notes _____

_____

"Friendship is a living thing that lasts only as long as it is nourished with kindness, sympathy, and understanding" (Anonymous).

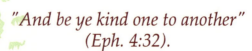

"And be ye kind one to another"
(Eph. 4:32).

Just for My Friend COUPON

A Walk-In-The-Mall Coupon.
The holder of this coupon is entitled to a Saturday afternoon of window-shopping with me in the mall of your choice. A surprise gift awaits you!

My personal gift to _____ From _____

Special notes _____

_____

"Friendships will last if they are put first" (Anonymous).

"Walk in love"
(Eph. 5:2).

I-Want-To-Help-You Coupon. *The holder of this coupon is entitled to my help with any project or special occasion that you are responsible for.*

Just for My Friend
COUPON

My personal gift to _____ From _____

Special notes _____

_____

"A true friend is like a good book –
the inside is better than the cover"
(Anonymous).

"With good will doing service, as to the Lord"
(Eph. 6:7).

Just for My Friend COUPON

The Open-Door Coupon. *The holder of this coupon is entitled to come to my home at any time, for any reason.*

My personal gift to _____ From _____

Special notes _____

_____

"A trusted friend thinks you are a good egg – even though you may be slightly cracked" (Anonymous).

"Submitting yourselves one to another in the fear of God" (Eph. 5:21).

Just for My Friend
COUPON

The You-Are-Important-To-Me Coupon. *The holder of this coupon is entitled to know that I consider you to be a very special person whom I believe in and enjoy being with.*

My personal gift to _____ From _____

Special notes _____

_____

"The best thing one friend can do for another is to refrain from giving advice" (Anonymous).

"Grace and peace be multiplied unto you through the knowledge of God" (2 Pet. 1:2).

Just for My Friend COUPON

Soft-Shoulder Coupon. *The holder of this coupon is entitled to the use of my shoulder to lean on or cry on during any time of personal crisis.*

My personal gift to _____ From _____

Special notes _____

_____

"The ornaments of a house
are the friends who frequent it"
(Anonymous).

*"Bear ye one another's burdens,
and so fulfil the law of Christ"
(Gal. 6:2).*

The Prayer-Support Coupon. *The holder of this coupon is entitled to my prayer support in any area of personal need you would like me to pray about. Your prayer request:*

_____
_____

Just for My Friend
COUPON

My personal gift to _____ From _____

Special notes _____

_____

"God never tires of hearing us in prayer" (Anonymous).

"But my God shall supply all your need according to his riches in glory by Christ Jesus" (Phil. 4:19).

Just for My Friend COUPON

The Weekend-Visit Coupon. *The holder of this coupon, and your family, are entitled to spend the weekend with me and my family on a mutually agreed-upon weekend in the near future. It will be a weekend of pure fun!*

My personal gift to _____ From _____

Special notes _____

_____

"Whatever you want to do, do it now.
There are only so many tomorrows"
(Michael Landon).

"And whatsoever ye do in word or deed, do all in the name of the Lord Jesus, giving thanks to God and the Father by him" (Col. 3:17).

The Encouragement Coupon. *I want to let you know I'll always be there for you, and I hope these words bring encouragement to you:*

_____
_____
_____

Just for My Friend
COUPON

My personal gift to _____ From _____

Special notes _____

_____

"The world is extremely interesting to a joyful soul" (Alexandra Stoddard).

"And be ye kind one to another, tenderhearted, forgiving one another, even as God for Christ's sake hath forgiven you" (Eph. 4:32).

Just for My Friend COUPON

The Please-Let-Me-Know-How-I-Can-Help Coupon. *The holder of this coupon is entitled to my commitment of personal help in any way that I can best serve you.*

My personal gift to _____ From _____

Special notes _____

_____

"Service is nothing but love in work clothes" (Anonymous).

"And above all these things put on charity [love], which is the bond of perfectness" (Col. 3:14).

__A Coupon Of Affirmation.__ The holder of this coupon is entitled to know that I think you are a very special person because:

_____

_____

Just for My Friend
COUPON

My personal gift to _____ From _____

Special notes _____

_____

"Love is the fairest flower that blooms in God's garden" (Anonymous).

"For it is God which worketh in you both to will and to do of his good pleasure" (Phil. 2:13).

Just for My Friend COUPON

The TLC Coupon. *The holder of this coupon is entitled to my "tender, loving care" when you are not feeling well.*

My personal gift to _____ From _____

Special notes _____

_____

"The first wealth is health"
(Ralph Waldo Emerson).

"But we have this treasure in earthen vessels, that the excellency of the power may be of God, and not of us"
(2 Cor. 4:7).

The Quiet Solitude Coupon. *The holder of this coupon is entitled to an evening of personal time away from your responsibilities. I will "hold down the fort" for you.*

Just for My Friend COUPON

My personal gift to _____ From _____

Special notes _____

_____

"There are voices which we hear in solitude, but they grow faint and inaudible as we enter into the world" (Ralph Waldo Emerson).

"Thou wilt keep him in perfect peace, whose mind is stayed on thee: because he trusteth in thee" (Isa. 26:3).

Just for My Friend COUPON

The I'll-Bring-You-A-Home-Cooked Meal Coupon. *The holder of this coupon is entitled to a home-cooked meal brought from my kitchen to your home. Choose your menu here:*

_____
_____.

My personal gift to _____ From _____

Special notes _____

_____

"Hospitality is one form of worship"
(The Talmud).

"I am that bread of life"
(Jesus — John 6:48).

The Invitation-To-Sunday-Dinner Coupon. *The holder of this coupon (and your family) are entitled to join me and my family for Sunday dinner on*

_____.

(RSVP by Saturday.)

Just for My Friend
COUPON

My personal gift to _____ From _____

Special notes _____

_____

"The table is a meeting place, a gathering ground, the source of sustenance and nourishment, festivity, safety, and satisfaction" (Laurie Colwin).

"But the fruit of the Spirit is love, joy, peace, longsuffering, gentleness, goodness, faith, Meekness, temperance: against such there is no law" (Gal. 5:22-23).

Just for My Friend
COUPON

The Guest-Of-Honor Coupon. *The holder of this coupon is entitled to be the guest of honor at a party I am throwing for you.*

Location: (my home)_____

Time: ____PM. You are in for a surprise!

My personal gift to _____ From _____

Special notes _____

_____

"Taking joy in life is a woman's best cosmetic"
(Rosalind Russell).

"And these things write we unto you,
that your joy may be full"
(1 John 1:4).

The I'll-Help-You-Cook Coupon.
The holder of this coupon is entitled to my personal assistance in the preparation of a special meal.

Just for My Friend
COUPON

My personal gift to _____ From _____

Special notes _____

_____

"It's difficult to think anything but pleasant thoughts while eating a home-grown tomato" (Lewis Grizzard).

"Fulfil ye my joy, that ye be like-minded, having the same love, being of one accord, of one mind" (Phil. 2:2).

Just for My Friend
COUPON

The Friend-For-Life Commitment Coupon. *The holder of this coupon is entitled to know that I covenant to be your friend for life. I want to always be there for you.*

My personal gift to _____ From _____

Special notes _____

_____

"Our aspirations are our possibilities"
(Samuel Johnson).

"Finally, be ye all of one mind, having compassion one of another, love as brethren,...be courteous" (1 Pet. 3:8).

Just for My Friend COUPON

The I'm-Thinking-About-You Coupon. *The holder of this coupon is entitled to know that I'm thinking about you, and hoping that all is well for you and yours. This is my prayer for you today:* _____.

My personal gift to _____ From _____

Special notes _____

_____

"To affect the quality of the day,
that is the highest of arts"
(Henry David Thoreau).

"And walk in love, as Christ also hath loved us,
and hath given himself for us an offering and a sacrifice
to God for a sweet-smelling savour"
(Eph. 5:2).

Just for My Friend COUPON

The Prayer-Support Coupon. *The holder of this coupon is entitled to my prayer support at all times. What specific prayer requests do you have?*

_____

_____

My personal gift to _____ From _____

Special notes _____

_____

"More things are wrought by prayer than this world dreams of" (Alfred, Lord Tennyson).

"Pray without ceasing. In every thing give thanks: for this is the will of God in Christ Jesus concerning you" (1 Thess. 5:17-18).

The Gratitude Coupon. *The holder of this coupon is entitled to know that I treasure our friendship. I appreciate you so much because:*_____ _____.

Just for My Friend
COUPON

My personal gift to _____ From _____

Special notes _____

_____

"Friends are people who help you be more yourself, more the person you are intended to be" (Merle Shain).

"We took sweet counsel together, and walked unto the house of God in company"
(Ps. 55:14).

Just for My Friend COUPON

The Christmas-Decoration Coupon. *The holder of this coupon is entitled to my help with decorating your home for Christmas. (I have a special decoration for you that I'll bring with me.)*

My personal gift to _____ From _____

Special notes _____

_____

"Giving presents is a talent; to know what a person wants, to know when and how to give it, to give it lovingly and well" (Pamela Glenconner).

"For God so loved the world, that he gave his only begotten Son, that whosoever believeth in him should not perish, but have everlasting life" (John 3:16).

Just for My Friend
COUPON

The Home-Bakery Coupon. *The holder of this coupon is entitled to spend a Saturday afternoon in my kitchen as we bake cookies and pies together. (I'll supply all the ingredients!)*

My personal gift to _____ From _____

Special notes _____

_____

"The body must be nourished, physically, emotionally and spiritually. We're spiritually starved in this culture – not underfed but undernourished" (Carol Hornig).

"The fear of the Lord is the beginning of wisdom"
(Ps. 111:10).

Just for My Friend COUPON

The Weekend-Away Coupon. *The holder of this coupon is entitled to spend a weekend away with me. We'll take time to rest, have fun, and enjoy life.*

My personal gift to _____ From _____

Special notes _____

_____

"Life is either a daring adventure or nothing. To keep our faces toward change and behave like free spirits in the presence of fate is strength undefeatable" (Helen Keller).

"That their hearts might be comforted, being knit together in love, and unto all riches of the full assurance of understanding, to the acknowledgement of the mystery of God, and of the Father, and of Christ" (Col. 2:2).

Just for My Friend COUPON

The You-Can-Do-It Coupon. *The holder of this coupon is entitled to know that I believe in your ability to accomplish what you have to do. I believe you can do it because:*

_____
_____ .

My personal gift to _____ From _____

Special notes _____

_____

"The conflict between what one is and who one is expected to be touches all of us. And sometimes . . . we choose the comfort of the failed role, preferring to be . . . the person who didn't have a chance" (Merle Shain).

"I can do all things through Christ which strengtheneth me" (Phil. 4:13).

Just for My Friend COUPON

The Fun Coupon. *The holder of this coupon is entitled to join me in an afternoon of fun. We'll do those things you enjoy most. (Nothing of a serious nature is permitted!)*

My personal gift to _____ From _____

Special notes _____

_____

"I would like to learn, or remember, how to live" (Annie Dillard).

"If they obey and serve him, they shall spend their days in prosperity, and their years in pleasures" (Job 36:11).

Just for My Friend COUPON

The Book Coupon. *The holder of this coupon is entitled to receive from me a book of your choice – the book you've most been wanting to read. The title and author are:*

_____
_____.

My personal gift to _____ From _____

Special notes _____

_____

"Only the heart knows how to find what is precious"
(Fyodor Dostoyevsky).

"Blessed shalt thou be when thou comest in,
and blessed shalt thou be when thou goest out"
(Deut. 28:6).

Just for My Friend COUPON

The Music-Therapy Coupon. *The holder of this coupon is entitled to receive from me a musical tape or CD of your choice. Your choice is:*

_____.

My personal gift to _____ From _____

Special notes _____

_____

"I think I should have no other mortal wants, if I could always have plenty of music. Life seems to go on without effort, when I am filled with music" (George Eliot).

*"Praise him with the sound of the trumpet:
praise him with the psaltery and harp"
(Ps. 150:3).*

The Garden Coupon. *The holder of this coupon is entitled to my help with any gardening project that is facing you.*

Just for My Friend
COUPON

My personal gift to _____ From _____

Special notes _____

_____

"Bloom where you're planted"
(Mary Engelbrett).

"Beloved, I wish above all things that thou mayest prosper and be in health, even as thy soul prospereth"
(3 John 2).

Just for My Friend
COUPON

The Interior-Decorating Coupon.
The holder of this coupon is entitled to my help with painting, wallpapering, or any other project involved with redecorating your home.

My personal gift to _____ From _____

Special notes _____

_____

"Have nothing in your homes that you do not know to be useful and believe to be beautiful" (William Morris).

"And to godliness brotherly kindness; and to brotherly kindness charity. For if these things be in you, and abound, they make you that ye shall neither be barren nor unfruitful in the knowledge of our Lord Jesus Christ" (2 Pet. 1:7-8).

Just for My Friend COUPON

The Basket-Of-Love Coupon.
The holder of this coupon is entitled to receive from me a basket full of the special things you like most.

My personal gift to _____ From _____

Special notes _____

_____

"Beauty is altogether in the eyes of the beholder" (Margaret Wolfe Hungerford).

"But speaking the truth in love, may grow up into him in all things, which is the head, even Christ" (Eph. 4:15).

Just for My Friend COUPON

The Aroma Coupon. *The holder of this coupon is entitled to receive from me a basket full of sweet-smelling things that will bring fragrance into your life.*

My personal gift to _____ From _____

Special notes _____

"Smells are surer than sounds and sights
to make heartstrings crack"
(Rudyard Kipling).

*"Now the God of hope fill you with all joy and
peace in believing, that ye may abound in hope"
(Rom. 15:13).*

Just for My Friend
COUPON

The Pleasant-Bath Coupon. *The holder of this coupon is entitled to receive from me bathing accessories that will bring greater relaxation and peace into your life.*

My personal gift to _____ From _____

Special notes _____

_____

"There must be quite a few things a hot bath won't cure, but I don't know many of them" (Sylvia Plath).

"He shall enter into peace: they shall rest in their beds, each one walking in his uprightness" (Isa. 57:2).

Just for My Friend
COUPON

The Theater Coupon. *The holder of this coupon is entitled to an evening at the theater with me. You choose the performance you would like to attend, and I will buy the tickets!*

My personal gift to _____ From _____

Special notes _____

_____

"The good life is waiting for us – here and now" (B.F. Skinner).

"The God of love and peace shall be with you" (2 Cor. 13:11).

Just for My Friend
C O U P O N

The Cookbook Coupon. *The holder of this coupon is entitled to receive from me the cookbook of your choice. (I will include my favorite recipe!)*

My personal gift to _____ From _____

Special notes _____

_____

"No one who cooks cooks alone. Even at her most solitary, a cook in the kitchen is surrounded by generations of cooks past, the advice and menus of cooks present, the wisdom of cookbook writers" (Laurie Colwin).

"Great peace have they which love thy law: and nothing shall offend them"
(Ps. 119:165).

The Sunshine Coupon. *The holder of this coupon is entitled to a day in the sunshine with me – at the pool, the park, the beach, or the lake.*

Just for My Friend
COUPON

My personal gift to _____ From _____

Special notes _____

_____

"Summer's lease hath all too short a date" (William Shakespeare).

"But the meek shall inherit the earth; and shall delight themselves in the abundance of peace" (Ps. 37:11).

Just for My Friend COUPON

The Candlelight Dinner Coupon.
The holder of this coupon (and your family) are entitled to attend a candlelight dinner at my home on _____ at _____PM. RSVP.

My personal gift to _____ From _____

Special notes _____

_____

"There are only two ways to live your life. One is as though nothing is a miracle. The other is as though everything is a miracle" (Albert Einstein).

"For the kingdom of God is not meat and drink; but righteousness, and peace, and joy in the Holy Ghost" (Rom. 14:17).

The Coupon Of Hope. *The holder of this coupon is entitled to receive these words of hope from me:*

_____
_____
_____.

Just for My Friend
COUPON

My personal gift to _____ From _____

Special notes _____

_____

"All shall be well, And all shall be well,
And all manner of things shall be well"
(Dame Julian of Norwich).

*"Now the God of hope fill you with all joy and peace
in believing, that ye may abound in hope,
through the power of the Holy Ghost"
(Rom. 15:13).*

Just for My Friend
COUPON

The Coupon Of Faith. *The holder of this coupon is entitled to know that God loves her, cares for her, watches over her, and keeps her. I write these words to build faith in your heart:*

_____
_____.

My personal gift to _____ From _____

Special notes _____

_____

"Fear falls before the fortress of faith" (Anonymous).

"Now faith is the substance of things hoped for, the evidence of things not seen" (Heb. 11:1).

The You-Are-Loved Coupon. *The holder of this coupon is entitled to know that you are greatly loved by God, me, and so many others. I want you to know how much you are loved, because:*

_____.

Just for My Friend
COUPON

My personal gift to _____ From _____

Special notes _____

_____

"This will be a better world when the power of love replaces the love of power" (Anonymous).

"The only thing that counts is faith expressing itself through love" (Gal. 5:6, NIV).

Just for My Friend COUPON

The Believe-In-Yourself Coupon.
The holder of this coupon is entitled to know that you are a wonderful person who has already accomplished great things, such as:

_____
_____. *(I believe in you!)*

My personal gift to _____ From _____

Special notes _____

_____

"You must first be a believer
if you would be an achiever"
(Anonymous).

"That the trial of your faith, being much more precious than of gold that perisheth, though it be tried with fire, might be found unto praise and honour and glory at the appearing of Jesus Christ"
(1 Pet. 1:7).

Just for My Friend
COUPON

The Happy-Birthday Coupon.
The holder of this coupon is entitled to know that you and I are going to have a special celebration of your birthday together. What would you like to do on your special day?

_____

My personal gift to _____ From _____

Special notes _____

_____

"The design on a woman's birthday cake is often very beautiful, but the arithmetic is terrible" (Anonymous).

"Rejoice with joy unspeakable and full of glory"
(1 Pet. 1:8).

Just for My Friend COUPON

The Diet-And-Exercise Coupon.
The holder of this coupon is entitled to know that I will join you in any diet-and-exercise program you choose. Let's encourage each other!

My personal gift to _____ From _____

Special notes _____

_____

"To feel 'fit as a fiddle' you must tone down your middle" (Anonymous).

"According to your faith be it unto you"
(Matt. 9:29).

The Weed-Your-Garden Coupon.
The holder of this coupon is entitled to my personal assistance in the weeding of your garden. (I'll bring my own hoe!)

Just for My Friend
COUPON

My personal gift to _____ From _____

Special notes _____

_____

"I'd rather have roses on my table,
than diamonds on my neck"
(Emma Goldman).

"The grace of our Lord Jesus Christ be with you"
(Rom. 16:20).

Just for My Friend COUPON

The Help-To-Get-Started Coupon.
The holder of this coupon is entitled to my personal assistance in getting a personal project that is important to you "off the ground."

My personal gift to _____ From _____

Special notes _____

_____

"Explore daily the will of God"
(Carl Jung).

*"Thy word is a lamp unto my feet,
and a light unto my path"
(Ps. 119:105).*

Just for My Friend COUPON

The You-Are-Never-Alone Coupon.
The holder of this coupon is entitled to know that God and I will never leave you nor forsake you. Even though miles may separate us, I will be there for you.

My personal gift to _____ From _____

Special notes _____

_____

"Many people are lonely because they build walls and not bridges" (Anonymous).

"Trust in the Lord with all thine heart; and lean not unto thine own understanding. In all thy ways acknowledge him, and he shall direct thy paths" (Prov. 3:5-6).

Just for My Friend COUPON

The Breakfast-In-Bed Coupon. *The holder of this coupon is entitled to a complimentary full breakfast (in bed) prepared by me. Delivery at sun-up. Rise and Shine! Your menu please:*

_____
_____

My personal gift to _____ From _____

Special notes _____

_____

"The early bird catches the worm"
(Ben Franklin).

"They are new every morning: great is thy faithfulness"
(Lam. 3:23).

It's-In-The-Bag Coupon. *The holder of this coupon is entitled to a day off from grocery shopping. You prepare the list and I'll pick up and deliver the goods. Do you prefer paper or plastic?*

Just for My Friend
COUPON

My personal gift to _____ From _____

Special notes _____

_____

"The greatest wonder of friendship is that the more you give, the richer you grow" (Anonymous).

"He shall feed his flock like a shepherd" (Isa. 40:11).

Just for My Friend COUPON

The Burden-Sharing Coupon. *The holder of this coupon is entitled to my help in resolving any issue you are facing.*

My personal gift to _____ From _____

Special notes _____

"Friendship is the only cement that will hold the world together" (Anonymous).

"Bear ye one another's burdens, and so fulfil the law of Christ" (Gal. 6:2).

The Tea-And-Me Coupon. *The holder of this coupon is entitled to a quiet afternoon of tea and cookies in my home with me.*

Just for My Friend
COUPON

My personal gift to _____ From _____

Special notes _____

_____

"The best vitamin for making friends is B-1" (Anonymous).

"The fruit of the Spirit is love"
(Gal. 5:22).

Just for My Friend COUPON

The Free-Luncheon Coupon. *The holder of this coupon is entitled to join me for lunch in our favorite restaurant on a mutually convenient day.*

My personal gift to _____ From _____

Special notes _____

_____

"Diet is best defined as a short period of starvation followed by a gain of five pounds!" (Anonymous).

"If we live in the Spirit, let us also walk in the Spirit" (Gal. 5:25).

The Movie-Matinee Coupon. *The holder of this coupon is entitled to select an afternoon movie that we can attend together. The movie and the popcorn are on me!*

Just for My Friend
COUPON

My personal gift to _____ From _____

Special notes _____

_____

"Friendship is a living thing that lasts only as long as it is nourished with kindness, sympathy, and understanding" (Anonymous).

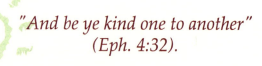

"And be ye kind one to another"
(Eph. 4:32).

Just for My Friend COUPON

The Fun Coupon. *The holder of this coupon is entitled to join me in an afternoon of fun. We'll do those things you enjoy most. (Nothing of a serious nature is permitted!)*

My personal gift to _____ From _____

Special notes _____

_____

"I would like to learn, or remember, how to live" (Annie Dillard).

"If they obey and serve him, they shall spend their days in prosperity, and their years in pleasures" (Job 36:11).

Coupon books from the *giftables*™ division of
Victory House Publishers:

Coupons of *Love* for *Married Couples*
Just for *My Friend* Coupons
Coupons of *Love* for *My Mom* — available Spring of 1998.
Coupons of *Love* for *My Dad* — available Spring of 1998.

Other books of interest available now!

- *A Little Bit of God's Wisdom & Wit*
- *A Little Bit of God's Wisdom & Wit for Women*
- *A Little Bit of God's Wisdom & Wit for Men*
- *Mini Prayers That Prevail*

See your local book or gift store, or call
Victory House Publishers at (918) 747-5009.

To Our Customers

Do you have a coupon idea? What special coupon would you like from a friend? If you send us a coupon idea that we use in future coupon books we will send you a free complimentary copy of the book your idea appears in. Your submission of a coupon idea implies your permission to use that idea free of charge in any and all future books. Send your coupon ideas to:

Victory House
Attn: Coupon Books
P.O. Box 700238
Tulsa, OK 74170